# DISCOVERING YOUR NICHE

The First Step to Business Success

JEFF C. COOK

# Table of Contents:

# Introduction

Finding one's specialty in the constantly changing world of entrepreneurship is like identifying the core of a flourishing company. Understanding the complex dance between a person's passion and market demand is essential in a world where innovation and specialization are at the top of the food chain. Welcome to "Discovering Your Niche: The First Step to Business Success," which offers a roadmap of the beginning stages that will direct you on the path of your entrepreneurial aspirations whether you are a beginning business professional looking to make your mark or an experienced business professional looking to diversify.

In these pages, we go in-depth on the art and science of finding the precise point where your interests and the demands of the market converge. This book is more than just a how-to guide; it's a transformational journey that enables you to reach your full potential and confidently negotiate the challenging landscape of entrepreneurship.

As you set out on your adventure, you'll research the importance of specialization and discover how it may serve as your compass in the huge commercial world. You will identify your interests, talents, and areas of competence through self-reflection and market research, then turn those things into successful companies. This book will show you how to create your brand, network with key mentors, and validate your ideas. Additionally, you will learn essential lessons on overcoming obstacles and developing resilience that will help you ensure that your firm not only survives but also thrives in the face of difficulty.

The case studies of prosperous businesspeople and the useful advice provided here will work as inspiration, illuminating your road to long-term economic success. Come along with us on this transforming adventure. Let's go out on a journey of self-discovery, market research, and company success together. Within these pages, your passion, niche, and success story are waiting.

# Chapter 1

# Understanding the Importance of a Niche

Understanding a niche emerges as the North Star directing entrepreneurs to success in the confusing world of business, where various products and services compete for attention. This chapter explores the significant relevance of knowing a niche, its definition, its significance, the benefits of operating in a niche market, and real-world examples of companies that have succeeded by embracing specialization.

## Defining a Niche: What it is and Why it Matters

A niche is, at its core, a specialized subset of the market, a particular subset distinguished by needs, preferences, or demographics. In contrast to the broad range of general markets, a niche is narrowly focused and serves a certain audience with similar interests or needs. This specificity is more than simply a market segment; it represents a strategic decision, allowing businesses to target their efforts, customize their products, and serve a target market with unmatched accuracy.

A niche's importance comes from its capacity to match consumer demand and individual enthusiasm. It serves as a link between what business owners enjoy doing and what customers are prepared to pay for. Businesses discover a responsive audience, an active network, and a platform to present their knowledge in a niche. Utilizing a powerful lens to focus on a certain market sector and get insights that are impossible to notice in the overall market landscape is analogous to understanding a niche.

# The Advantages of Operating Within a Niche Market

## Focused Expertise and Understanding

Businesses that operate in narrow markets might develop specialized knowledge and understanding. Businesses can deeply explore the specifics of their niche by focusing their efforts on a certain sector or consumer group. They can foresee industry trends, pinpoint specific consumer demands, and develop novel solutions that have a dramatic impact on their audience thanks to this depth of expertise. Niche firms grow to be experts in their field, providing unmatched knowledge and experience that sets them apart from rivals in larger marketplaces.

## Targeted Marketing and Messaging

Businesses may create tailored marketing strategies and communications by having a clear understanding of their niche. Businesses in a niche can develop campaigns that are specifically targeted to satisfy the issues and goals of their audience rather than using generic marketing strategies that frequently fall short. Customers respond favorably to this individualized strategy, which fosters engagement and emotional relationships. Niche firms can optimize their marketing initiatives to make sure that every message resonates with their niche audience, whether through social media, content marketing, or traditional advertising.

## Reduced Competition and Market Saturation

Businesses frequently find themselves submerged in fierce rivalry and market saturation in the huge sea of commerce. However, niche markets provide a haven from this competitive climate. Because they serve a narrow market, niche businesses have fewer direct rivals, which makes it easier for them to grow without being constantly pressured by pricing wars or aggressive marketing strategies. Because there is less rivalry, businesses can grow naturally by concentrating on providing top-notch goods or services and creating enduring bonds with their clients.

## Enhanced Customer Loyalty and Relationships

Customers feel more loyal and a sense of belonging when they are aware of their specialty. Businesses that customize their goods to satisfy the needs of a niche market have a special value proposition that has a strong emotional connection with customers. Customers are drawn to the personalization, which also helps to maintain their loyalty. Because they provide solutions that are perfectly tailored to their needs, niche enterprises frequently become indispensable aspects of their client's lives. As a result, clients inside a niche are more likely to stick around and develop into brand evangelists who ardently urge others to patronize the company.

## Flexibility and Adaptability

Niche firms are by nature flexible and adaptive. They can react quickly to alterations in market dynamics, consumer preferences, or technology breakthroughs because of their specific emphasis. The agility with which specialist enterprises may change their strategy, launch new goods, and respond to changing consumer preferences sets them apart from their larger, less specialized rivals. This adaptability is a valued quality, especially in fields where remaining on the cutting edge is crucial to survival. Because niche businesses may innovate and make changes quickly, they can stay competitive and relevant in the ever-changing business environment.

## Higher Profit Margins

Having more focus results in larger profit margins frequently. Customers in specialized markets are frequently willing to pay more for goods or services that specifically address their demands. Because of the special value they bring to their customers, niche enterprises can charge more for their products. A niche firm can concentrate on quality, innovation, and customer experience while larger businesses may need to compete largely on pricing. This allows niche businesses to maintain good profit margins while providing outstanding value to their clients.

## Innovation and Creativity

A culture of innovation and creativity is nurtured by understanding a niche. Businesses that operate in specialized markets are urged to think creatively and explore unconventional solutions to solve the unique problems their target market faces. This emphasis on innovation frequently results in the creation of ground-breaking goods or services that establish new standards for the industry. Without the restrictions of mass-market appeal, niche enterprises can push the envelope of innovation and develop products that are both innovative and highly functional. This innovative spirit not only appeals to a certain audience but also has the potential to influence a larger market, creating trends and developments that have a significant impact on the entire sector.

## Long-Term Sustainability

Long-term sustainability is ensured by understanding a niche. Due to their narrow focus and devoted clientele, niche businesses are frequently more immune to market volatility and economic downturns. Consumer behavior can change dramatically for enterprises in larger markets during difficult times, while specialized markets, which are characterized by devoted clients, tend to stay relatively steady. Even in times of economic uncertainty, customers in a niche are likely to remain loyal, ensuring a consistent flow of income for specialized enterprises. Additionally, the knowledge and reputation developed inside a certain industry serve as a barrier to entry for new rivals, preserving the company's position and assuring its long-term viability.

## Successful Niche Businesses

Dollar Shave Club

Dollar Shave Club, which Michael Dubin founded in 2011, upended the razor market by catering to a particular market segment: males seeking high-quality razors at competitive prices. Dollar Shave Club capitalized on the rising desire for practical and affordable shaving options by providing a membership service that shipped razors and grooming supplies right to consumers' doors. The business swiftly grew to have a huge following thanks to clever marketing and a keen understanding of its specialized market, and in 2016 Unilever bought it for $1 billion. The success of Dollar Shave Club serves as a testament to the value of specializing in one's goods to satisfy certain client demands.

Toms Shoes

Blake Mycoskie launched Toms Shoes in 2006, which is a perfect illustration of a company that is motivated by a social niche. Toms promised to provide a child in need a pair of shoes for each pair of shoes purchased. Customers who sought not only high-quality shoes but also a feeling of meaning in their purchases connected strongly with this socially conscious approach. Toms' dedication to social responsibility attracted a loyal consumer base and turned the business into a worldwide sensation. Toms Shoes gave an example of the transforming power of focusing on a niche market by identifying the market of socially aware customers and matching their business strategy with a worthwhile cause.

## CrossFit

Greg Glassman established CrossFit in 2000 to serve a particular market segment: people looking for intense, functional workouts. By fusing aspects of weightlifting, cardio, and bodyweight exercises, CrossFit set itself apart from the competition and provided a holistic fitness program that appealed to fans seeking a hard and interesting workout. CrossFit quickly attracted a fervent following because of its distinctive methodology and community-centered attitude, which resulted in the opening of several CrossFit facilities (or "boxes") all over the world. CrossFit became a global fitness sensation by recognizing the need for a more challenging and varied workout regimen among fitness enthusiasts, demonstrating the importance of specialization in recruiting devoted followers.

## MailChimp

In the field of email marketing, MailChimp, which was created by Ben Chestnut and Dan Kurzius in 2001, is a shining example of a successful niche company. MailChimp, which caters to small and medium-sized businesses, provides a user-friendly email marketing platform that enables companies to build, send, and track email campaigns. MailChimp has successfully cornered the market for entrepreneurs and small business owners looking for a hassle-free email marketing solution by emphasizing simplicity, affordability, and user-friendly features. MailChimp has established itself as the go-to option for companies with little marketing experience and resources thanks to its user-friendly interface and comprehensive features. MailChimp rose to the top of its field by recognizing the demand for affordable and efficient email marketing tools among small firms, demonstrating the tactical benefits of targeting a particular market.

## Nurturing Success through Niche Understanding

Knowing your niche is more than just a company strategy—it's the basis for turning your entrepreneurial aspirations into real-world triumphs. Businesses that understand the nuances of a certain niche in the connected global market open a world of potential. Businesses operating in a niche market transcend the ordinary and transform into extraordinary entities that thrive in the face of complexity by matching passion with market demand, customizing services to satisfy distinct needs, and cultivating close relationships with a committed audience.

Understanding a niche is a transforming process that requires business owners to delve deeply into customer needs, industry nuances, and market complexities. It's a journey that calls for compassion, imagination, and unflinching commitment. Customers' loyalty, colleagues' praise, and the lasting joy of having a significant influence are all rewards for those who set out on this voyage with an open mind and a good grasp of their audience.

Knowing your specialization in the business world is like discovering the ideal thread that will help you create a successful firm. It is more than just a thread; it is the shining golden filament that illuminates the road and directs organizations toward long-term prosperity, steadfast client loyalty, and sustainable growth. Let business owners and entrepreneurs embrace the profound wisdom of identifying a niche as they negotiate the difficulties of the contemporary marketplace. We are reminded that in the world of business, specificity is not a limitation; it is the key that unlocks limitless opportunities and propels us toward a future where success knows no bounds. Within the niche lies not only the promise of prosperity but also the fulfillment of entrepreneurial aspirations.

# Chapter 2

# Self-Discovery: Identifying Your Passions and Strengths

One of the basic cornerstones of creating a successful firm in the vast terrain of entrepreneurship, where innovation meets aspiration, is self-discovery. Understanding oneself is more than just a procedure; it's a transformational journey that can help people find their special place in the crowded market. This chapter digs deeply into the areas of self-discovery, examining the complexities of evaluating abilities, passions, and interests, identifying unique skills and knowledge, and unraveling the intriguing landscape where interests and hobbies transform into successful businesses.

## Assessing Your Skills, Interests, and Passions: The Core of Self-Discovery

A thorough evaluation of one's abilities, passions, and interests constitutes the first step on the journey to self-discovery. As a result of education, training, and experience, people develop skills—tangible abilities and capabilities. Passions are the ingrained feelings that stoke zeal and drive, whereas interests are the subjects of wonder and fascination. Examining these facets of oneself is like scouting out the area before setting off on a voyage. It offers clarity by emphasizing areas of competence, passion, and room for improvement.

Skill Assessment: Think about your personal and professional strengths. Consider your training, employment history, credentials, and any specialty certificates you may have. List both hard talents (technical aptitudes connected to certain activities) and soft skills (leadership, interpersonal, and communication qualities). Examine not only your knowledge but also your openness to lifelong learning and change.

Interests Exploration: Consider your interests outside of work. Think about the themes, hobbies, or things that pique your interest. These passions can include everything from literature and the arts to technology and societal issues. Keep an eye out for things that cause you to lose track of time, as these occasions frequently disclose your true interests.

Passions Unveiling: Explore your interests, those underlying feelings that give you energy and drive. What problems or causes stoke your passion? What pursuits or objectives make you feel alive? A sense of purpose is frequently associated with passion, which can offer priceless insights into prospective company concepts that are consistent with your basic values.

## Recognizing Your Unique Strengths and Expertise

Understanding your talents and areas of competence is a crucial part of self-discovery; it goes beyond merely acknowledging your skills and interests. These characteristics are the parts of your personality and skills that make you unique. Finding these qualities is like finding hidden jewels within yourself that can show you the way to a successful and fulfilling specialty.

Strengths Recognition: Consider your assets, such as fortitude, originality, flexibility, empathy, and problem-solving skills. Consider the supportive comments you have had from mentors, friends, and coworkers. These characteristics are innate strengths that influence how you respond to difficulties and opportunities rather than merely being skills.

Expertise Acknowledgement: Determine your specialty areas. These are the areas where you excel, the disciplines you are an expert in or the abilities you have developed over time. Both broad and specific expertise are possible. You might, for instance, be an expert in marketing in general or in digital advertising specifically. You may effectively use your expertise in your entrepreneurial path if you acknowledge it.

## Exploring How Your Hobbies and Interests Can Turn into Profitable Ventures

One of the most intriguing aspects of self-discovery is realizing that your interests and hobbies may go beyond just being something you do for fun and become successful businesses. Innovative ideas are created at the nexus of passion and entrepreneurship when interests are transformed into flourishing businesses.

<u>Identifying Profitable Hobbies</u>: Examine your interests and hobbies more closely. While some hobbies may appear to be personal or leisure pursuits, they frequently have hidden business potential. If you like to plant, for instance, you might explore the niche market for organic gardening supplies. If you enjoy making, your works might serve as the basis for an internet shop selling handcrafted goods. Finding the potential for profit in your interests needs both innovation and market study.

<u>Market Research and Validation</u>: Once you've found possible business ventures arising from your passions, thoroughly research the market. Look into the market demand for goods and services in your niche. Analyze the tastes and purchasing patterns of your target market. To verify your theories, take part in surveys, interviews, and online research. The link between enthusiasm and financial success is market validation, which confirms that there is a need for your products.

<u>Innovation and Differentiation</u>: Finding several revenue streams within your expertise is the first step in monetizing your interest. For instance, if you have a passion for fitness, you may design fitness apparel, build fitness-related apps, offer personal training sessions, and make online fitness courses. Your business will be financially stable and sustainable if you diversify your sources of income. Additionally, looking into collaborations, partnerships, and sponsorships in your area may reveal new opportunities for money generation.

# Case Studies of Turning Passions into Profitable Ventures.

## Etsy: Empowering Artisans and Crafts

The online marketplace Etsy, which was established in 2005, is a prime example of how to turn interests into successful businesses. The portal caters to artists, crafters, and vintage enthusiasts and focuses on handcrafted or unusual things. Crafting, painting, and vintage item collecting became popular worldwide thanks to Etsy. Etsy transformed interests and artistic passions into a successful business model by offering a forum for sellers to promote their works and connect with customers who share their interests. Millions of craftsmen and artisans use Etsy today to commercialize their artistic abilities, demonstrating the enormous potential in niche marketplaces for hobbies and skills.

## MasterClass: Learning from the Best

An online learning platform called MasterClass was established in 2015 and provides courses instructed by well-known specialists and celebrities. The portal offers content on a wide range of subjects, including writing, music, and filmmaking. MasterClass capitalizes on the enthusiasm people have for studying under luminaries they respect. MasterClass built a successful business by turning the knowledge and enthusiasm of well-known people into online courses that appeal to the interests and curiosities of students all around the world. The platform shows the potential of transforming knowledge and passion into a successful educational platform by not only monetizing the desire for information but also by offering a distinctive and immersive learning experience.

<u>Airbnb: Sharing the Passion for Travel and Hospitality</u>

By capitalizing on people's desire for travel and cultural encounters, Airbnb launched in 2008, changed the tourism and hospitality sectors. People can use the platform to hire distinctive lodging and activities provided by neighborhood hosts. Airbnb transformed a love of hospitality and travel into a successful peer-to-peer business. While guests indulge their love for unique experiences, hosts make money off their extra rooms, vacation properties, or local knowledge. Airbnb is a prime example of how a successful business model can be built on a person's enthusiasm for travel and cultural immersion. Airbnb has succeeded by turning this passion into a global marketplace.

## The Transformative Power of Self-Discovery

Self-discovery is a constant process that drives creativity, enthusiasm, and long-term progress throughout the entrepreneurial path rather than just a first step. Entrepreneurs can find their niche, a special area where personal fulfillment and financial success collide, by understanding their abilities, interests, and passions. Entrepreneurs are better able to use their intrinsic skills to enhance their offers and value propositions when they are aware of their strengths and expertise. Furthermore, learning how passions and hobbies may be turned into successful businesses offers up a world of imaginative possibilities where passion becomes the engine of prosperous businesses.

The case studies of Etsy, MasterClass, and Airbnb provide excellent examples of how self-discovery may transform. These platforms created ecosystems where passions, creativity, and skill may flourish in addition to enterprises. They took hold of people's intrinsic interests, whether they be for learning, exploring, or making things, and made them into widespread occurrences. These instances highlight the tremendous benefits of fusing one's interests with entrepreneurial endeavors, resulting in businesses that connect with clients on a deep level and endure over time.

Self-discovery is the colorful thread that gives the entrepreneurial story color and depth in the tapestry of entrepreneurship. Businesses are given character, creativity, and purpose by the essence. The essence of each aspiring entrepreneur's specific niche may be found deep inside their abilities, interests, and passions; thus, it is imperative that they fully embrace the process as they set out on their road to self-discovery. It is a journey that goes beyond the ordinary, turning aspirations into accomplishments and dreams into real, successful businesses. Self-discovery helps business owners not only identify their market niches but also their true selves, resulting in the creation of enterprises that are not only successful but also profoundly gratifying.

# Chapter 3

# Market Research: Identifying Profitable Opportunities

Market research serves as a guiding light for business owners, pointing them in the direction of untapped opportunities and lucrative niches in the ever-evolving business landscape. The stepping stones of insight, comprehension, and anticipation—components that are painstakingly created through extensive market research—are used to pave the path to entrepreneurial success. This chapter digs deeply into the complex world of market research, examining the complexities of carrying out exhaustive studies, examining trends and market gaps, and figuring out the complex wants and pain points of the target market. Market research becomes the lynchpin on which lucrative chances are located and entrepreneurial aspirations are translated into successful businesses by illuminating these routes.

## Conducting Thorough Market Research: The Foundation of Niche Discovery

The methodical process of obtaining, examining, and interpreting data on a market, including its potential clients and rivals, is known as market research. It is a constant practice, not just an initial step, that guides important company decisions and guarantees that business owners are knowledgeable and flexible in their thinking. A range of approaches and procedures are used in thorough market research to obtain comprehensive insights.

Primary Research Methods: Primary research is gathering authentic data directly from the source. Surveys, interviews, focus groups, and observations can all be used to this end. Surveys are organized questionnaires that are given to a sample of participants and provide quantitative information. Entrepreneurs can delve deeply into the thoughts, opinions, and preferences of participants through focus groups and interviews, which provide qualitative information. An important backdrop for decision-making is provided by observational research, which entails studying consumer behavior in real-world situations.

Secondary Research Sources: Gathering existing data for secondary research entails consulting government publications, academic journals, business periodicals, and market reports. These sources provide a plethora of knowledge regarding economic indicators, rival strategy, consumer behavior, and market trends. Primary research is complemented by secondary research, which offers a more comprehensive view of the market environment.

Online Analytics and Social Media Listening: Through web analytics and social media platforms, the digital age has brought us an influx of a multitude of data. Insights into user behavior, website traffic, and conversion rates are provided by website analytics. Entrepreneurs can monitor online conversations, sentiments, and trends relating to their industry or specialty using social media listening tools. Entrepreneurs can receive immediate insights into market dynamics and customer preferences by utilizing these digital technologies.

## Analyzing Trends and Gaps in the Market: Navigating the Shifting Sands of Commerce

The goal of market research is to uncover unmet requirements and anticipate future trends in addition to analyzing the industry's current situation. It takes a keen eye for developing patterns and a thorough understanding of customer behavior to analyze trends and gaps in the market. Entrepreneurs need to anticipate adjustments in consumer demand, technology developments, and societal trends that can affect their market.

Identifying Emerging Trends: Entrepreneurs can spot new trends by examining customer behavior and market data currently available. These trends might be influenced by changes in technology, fashion, the environment, or culture. For instance, a rise in eco-conscious consumerism has been sparked by consumers' increasing preference for sustainable goods and environmentally beneficial behaviors. Entrepreneurs who are aware of these trends and who adapt to them might position their companies as market leaders in new markets.

Exploring Market Gaps: Unmet needs or underserved market segments are represented by market gaps. It takes a careful examination of current goods, services, and consumer experiences to spot these gaps. Entrepreneurs must carefully examine consumer testimonials, comments, and pain concerns to identify gaps in the current products. A market gap could present chances for novel solutions, improved consumer experiences, or game-changing company strategies. Successful businesspeople understand that gaps are not barriers, but rather openings for innovative problem-solving and specialist research.

Technological Innovations and Disruptions: The development of technology has the potential to transform entire sectors. Entrepreneurs need to keep a close eye on technical advancements and industry upheavals. The emergence of blockchain technology, AI, and the Internet of Things (IoT) has transformed industries as diverse as finance and healthcare. By utilizing these technologies, business owners can develop ground-breaking solutions that satisfy changing customer needs and market demands.

## Identifying Target Audience Needs and Pain Points: The Heartbeat of Entrepreneurial Success

Entrepreneurial success begins with an understanding of the demands and problems of the target market. Entrepreneurs must understand their consumers' needs and goals by putting themselves in their customers' shoes. Entrepreneurs may adapt their offers, develop compelling value propositions, and build sincere relationships with their clients by recognizing these demands and pain spots.

**Empathetic Listening and Surveys:** Engaging with clients directly, getting their input, and truly comprehending their experiences are all part of empathic listening. It is possible to craft surveys and questionnaires to elicit certain replies about the preferences, degrees of satisfaction, and pain areas of customers. Entrepreneurs can learn a lot about areas that need development or innovation by listening to their customers.

**Customer Journey Mapping:** Customer journey mapping represents the interactions, feelings, and experiences that a customer has with a brand at multiple touchpoints. Entrepreneurs can pinpoint pain areas, bottlenecks, and moments of joy or annoyance by mapping the client's journey. With the help of this visual representation, business owners may improve customer happiness and solve problem issues.

**Social Media Engagement and Reviews:** Platforms for social media act as hubs for customer conversations. Through social media platforms, business owners may interact with clients directly and respond to their questions, concerns, and feedback. Online reviews on sites like Yelp, Google, or Amazon offer direct information on customer experiences. Entrepreneurs can get knowledge from both good and negative feedback by identifying areas for development and understanding of the target market.

# Niche Opportunities Discovered through Market Research

## Beyond Meat: Tapping into Plant-Based Revolution

Ethan Brown launched Beyond Meat in 2009, and it is a shining example of a business that recognized a market need and capitalized on new trends. Beyond Meat undertook comprehensive market research to comprehend consumer tastes and dietary choices to meet the growing need for meat substitutes made from plants. The business created plant-based meat replacements that closely resemble the flavor and texture of animal-based proteins by utilizing scientific innovation. Beyond Meat established itself as a pioneer in the expanding plant-based food sector by capitalizing on the popularity of plant-based diets and meeting the demand for sustainable, ecologically friendly substitutes. With careful market research, the business not only discovered a market gap but also developed a revolutionary niche that is in line with changing customer values.

## Peleton: Revolutionizing Home Fitness

John Foley established Peloton in 2012, making it a pioneer in the home fitness sector. The business recognized a need in the market for easy and engaging at-home workouts. According to Peloton's market research, there is a rising market of consumers looking for fitness products that provide the advantages of personal training and group exercise in the convenience of their own homes. Peloton created a variety of linked fitness gadgets, such as stationary bikes and treadmills, in conjunction with live and on-demand training sessions by utilizing technology and content production. Peloton carved out a niche that appeals to busy professionals, fitness lovers, and people looking for convenient training solutions by addressing the need for engaging, high-quality home fitness experiences.

## Zoom Video Communications: Enabling Remote Collaboration

Eric Yuan launched Zoom Video Communications in 2011 after realizing the growing trend of remote work and the demand for flawless virtual communication solutions. The company recognized the difficulties that people and businesses encounter when conducting remote meetings and cooperation through in-depth market research. Zoom addressed the drawbacks of conventional communication tools with its user-friendly design, dependable video conferencing, and collaboration features. Zoom fulfilled the immediate demands of organizations by providing a platform that facilitates remote collaboration, but it also foresaw the long-term trend toward remote work. The company's success reflects its capacity to recognize market trends, comprehend user needs, and provide solutions that consider the changing nature of work and communication.

# Market Research as the Catalyst of Niche Success

Market research is a dynamic process that changes along with market trends and consumer preferences in the world of entrepreneurship. Entrepreneurs can find lucrative opportunities, expand on current solutions, and develop game-changing niche businesses by conducting thorough research. Businesses are propelled beyond the world of conjecture thanks to market research, which enables business owners to make wise decisions based on verifiable facts and client feedback.

Entrepreneurs are better equipped to traverse the challenging landscape of business when they comprehend the subtleties of market research. It gives them the ability to foresee changes in demand, take advantage of new trends, and satisfy unmet consumer demands. The case studies of Beyond Meat, Peloton, and Zoom Video Communications highlight how market research can revolutionize an industry. These businesses didn't merely penetrate already-existing sectors; by seeing gaps, embracing trends, and satisfying customer needs, they changed entire industries.

Entrepreneurs must understand that market research will be their constant companion as they set out on their adventure to find their niche. The lantern is what sheds light on the shadows, uncovering hidden opportunities and directing people toward successful endeavors. Market research is not just a procedure; it is the strategic imperative that drives companies toward long-term success, making it an essential tool for business owners hoping to succeed in the dynamic commercial environment. Entrepreneurial dreams become attainable reality through the application of market research, resulting in companies that not only cater to the needs of the present but also foresee those of the future.

# Chapter 4

# Passion meets Profit:
# Aligning Your Passions with Market Demand

The meeting of individual passion and commercial desire is the fundamental junction of entrepreneurship. Businesses that combine their passions with financial success are no longer just endeavors; rather, they represent imagination, commitment, and sincere fulfillment. This chapter launches into an engrossing investigation of the complex tango between market need and personal passion, revealing the art of balancing individual desires with the ever-evolving currents of consumer requirements. Entrepreneurs can embark on a transformative journey where passion becomes the driving force behind profitable, sustainable businesses by matching passions with market demands, brainstorming innovative business ideas rooted in genuine interests, and assessing the viability and profitability of these ideas.

## Matching Your Passions with Market Demands: The Harmony of Authenticity and Relevance

Integral to bringing passion and market demand together are authenticity and relevancy. Finding personal passions that are meaningful to both a target audience and the entrepreneur on a deep level is the art of entrepreneurship. The entrepreneur's excitement and knowledge infuse the company with authenticity because of this congruence and satisfying real consumer requirements and aspirations promotes relevance and market acceptance.

Reflective Self-Exploration: Deep self-reflection is the first step in bringing your passion and market demand together. Entrepreneurs need to look deeper into their passions than their obvious hobbies. What pursuits truly make you happy and fulfilled? What factors or problems stoke passion? An in-depth examination of oneself via reflection reveals passions that are not simply passing interests but enduring components of the entrepreneur's character.

Market Research and Gap Analysis: Entrepreneurs must simultaneously perform in-depth market research to spot any holes in the industry, unmet demands, or underserved groups. Market research identifies areas with significant consumer demand but few available options. Entrepreneurs can build companies that meet real needs by matching their passions with these found voids, ensuring a market for their goods or services.

Passion-Driven Purpose: A meaningful business is built on the confluence of passion and purpose. Entrepreneurs should consider how their passion might improve the lives of others. How can it improve experiences or solve challenges? Consumers have a strong affinity for companies that are driven by a strong sense of purpose and real passion. Passion turns into the guiding light that shows the way toward adding value and improving the lives of consumers.

# Brainstorming Business Ideas Based on Your Interests: Cultivating Innovation from Passionate Seeds

The process of coming up with company concepts based on personal interests is creative and results in the emergence of ground-breaking ideas. Entrepreneurs who want to find new perspectives and chances within their hobbies must adopt an attitude of curiosity, exploration, and open-mindedness.

Diverse Perspectives: Diverse viewpoints are beneficial during brainstorming sessions. Entrepreneurs can ask friends, mentors, or colleagues from a variety of backgrounds and experiences to join them. By challenging presumptions and considering unusual alternatives, diverse opinions frequently generate novel ideas. The idea is to distill the entrepreneur's passion and examine it from several perspectives.

Cross-Industry Inspiration: At the confluence of different sectors, inspiration frequently occurs. Entrepreneurs can make links between their interests and sectors that at first glance seem unconnected. For instance, combining technology with a love of storytelling could result in captivating virtual reality experiences. Entrepreneurs are encouraged to think outside of the box through cross-industry inspiration, which generates creative, hybrid business concepts.

Feedback and Iteration: Iterative brainstorming should be used to generate ideas. Entrepreneurs can ask focus groups, prospective clients, or reliable consultants for advice. The original notions can be improved and refined with the help of feedback. By encouraging adaptation, iterative brainstorming enables business owners to modify their concepts in response to customer feedback and shifting fashions.

## Evaluating the Feasibility and Profitability of Your Ideas: From Vision to Viable Business

A rigorous assessment of the viability and profitability of the ideas is necessary for the transition from creative brainstorming to a successful business. Passionate concepts must be thoroughly examined to make sure they are in line with market reality and have the potential to develop into long-lasting, lucrative businesses.

Market Validation: Testing the company concept in the actual market context is known as market validation. To get feedback from customers, entrepreneurs can develop prototypes, provide trial services, or release limited quantities. Customer contacts, sales data, and feedback offer verifiable proof of market demand. Early idea validation reduces risks and enables business owners to change their concepts in response to actual customer input.

Financial Viability: A crucial component of sustainable enterprises is financial viability. Entrepreneurs need to make thorough financial estimates, considering things like production costs, pricing tactics, operations expenditures, and income sources. Calculations of return on investment (ROI), break-even analysis, and cash flow forecasts offer insights into the financial health of the company. To secure profitability and long-term sustainability, entrepreneurs must make sure that their ardent pursuits are in line with good financial principles.

Scalability and Growth Potential: Long-term success requires assessing the business idea's scalability and growth potential. Entrepreneurs must determine whether the concept can be successfully scaled to meet rising demand without sacrificing quality or the consumer experience. Scalable business models make it possible for passionate projects to develop into successful businesses that can accommodate growth and expansion without encountering severe operational challenges.

## Examples of Passion-Driven Profitable Ventures

Warby Parker: Revolutionizing Eyewear with a Purpose

Neil Blumenthal, Dave Gilboa, Andrew Hunt, and Jeffrey Raider launched Warby Parker in 2010, and it is a prime example of how drive, purpose, and market demand can come together. Although the founders had a strong enthusiasm for eyewear, they were aware of the exorbitant costs and lack of transparency in the market. They turned their enthusiasm into a business concept: providing reasonably priced, fashionable eyewear while solving the problem of access to vision care. Customers could try on glasses at home thanks to Warby Parker's novel method, which eliminated the inconvenience of conventional in-store purchasing. Warby Parker not only satisfied market demand but also made a positive social impact by fusing their love of eyewear with a commitment to offer consumers cheap, accessible eyewear. The company's success is a testament to the power of aligning personal passion with a genuine societal need, creating a thriving business that resonates with customers and makes a positive difference.

## S'well: Satisfying the Thirst for Sustainability

Sarah Kauss founded S'well in 2010 because of her love of sustainability and dedication to lowering plastic waste. Sarah Kauss developed chic, reusable water bottles by fusing her passion for design with her concern for the environment. In addition to meeting the increased demand from customers for eco-friendly substitutes, S'well's goods featured cutting-edge designs and colorful aesthetics. Kauss developed a unique brand that met consumer needs while also promoting environmental preservation by fusing her enthusiasm for sustainability with the market's demand for eco-conscious goods. The success of S'well demonstrates the transforming power of matching one's passion with market demand, producing a successful business that appeals to socially conscious customers.

## The Alchemy of Passion and Profit

Entrepreneurs embark on a transforming journey where creativity meets commerce and personal fulfillment converges with market needs in the complex dance between passion and profit. Beyond the transactional character of business, the synthesis of passion and profit gives endeavors an authentic, enthusiastic, and sincere purpose. Entrepreneurs who match their interests with consumer needs build enterprises that are more than just profit-making endeavors; they are also manifestations of their creativity, inventiveness, and unrelenting commitment.

The alchemy of passion and profit is demonstrated by the case studies of Warby Parker, and S'well. Instead of merely identifying market gaps, these businesses transformed their emotions into game-changing concepts that struck a chord with customers. These business owners have built companies that surpassed conventional paradigms and had a long-lasting effect on their industry and customers by infusing them with purpose and authenticity.

Entrepreneurs must embrace the alchemical process that turns unadulterated enthusiasm into successful businesses as they explore the intersection of their passions and market demand. Self-reflection, empathy, creativity, and strategic thinking are all necessary during this process. Entrepreneurs need to be fearless visionaries who aren't scared to defy expectations and venture into unknown waters. They must see obstacles as learning opportunities and failures as opportunities to innovate.

Entrepreneurs discover the elixir that makes their dreams come true in the alchemy of passion and profit. It is a journey where inspiration comes from passion, the market drives innovation, and the union of self-fulfillment and customer happiness produces businesses that are not just profitable but also profoundly meaningful. The alchemy of passion and profit is not just a business plan; it is the essence that transforms enterprises into legacies, leaving an everlasting imprint on sectors, communities, and the entrepreneurial environment. As entrepreneurs set out on this transforming voyage, they must understand this. Through this profound alchemy, entrepreneurs not only discover their niche in the market but also create ventures that resonate with the very essence of their being, forging a path where passion and profit are not just partners but soulmates, crafting a legacy of enduring success and profound fulfillment.

# Chapter 5

# Skills Development: Bridging the Gap

Skills are the threads that connect goals and accomplishments in the complex tapestry of enterprise. The acquisition of knowledge and skills has a significant impact on the process of finding one's specialty in the corporate world. The goal of this essay is to illuminate the process of developing one's skills by defining the skills required for a certain specialty, investigating several possibilities for education and training, and acquiring real-world experience through internships and freelancing. Aspiring entrepreneurs can bridge the gap between their aspirations and competence through this transforming process, opening the door to significant contributions and long-term success in their industry.

## Identifying the Necessary Skills and Knowledge for Your Chosen Niche: The Foundation of Expertise

Every company specialization requires a particular set of abilities and information. Finding these fundamental qualities is the first step in mastering a certain field. Entrepreneurs must thoroughly examine their market and comprehend the technical, artistic, and management abilities necessary for success.

Industry Research and Competitor Analysis: The abilities of competitors and changing trends within the niche are revealed by thorough industry research and competition analysis. Entrepreneurs can determine the abilities that are appreciated and sought-after by looking at successful businesses in their chosen industry. This analysis acts as a compass, pointing people in the direction of learning the necessary abilities.

Networking and Mentorship: Engaging with experts and mentors in the industry provides opportunities to learn about its subtleties. Opportunities to engage with professionals and peers can be found at networking events, business conferences, and online forums. Mentors provide helpful advice by imparting their knowledge and expertise and frequently recommending skills that are essential for successfully navigating the profession.

Self-Assessment and Skill Gap Analysis: Entrepreneurial self-assessment entails assessing one's current abilities and determining any deficiencies. Self-aware entrepreneurs can identify development opportunities. Entrepreneurs should prioritize their learning process by employing skill gap analysis, concentrating on the most important abilities for their specialty. This introspective method makes sure that skill development is in line with individual preferences and market needs.

## Exploring Education and Training Options: Nurturing Expertise Through Learning

Skills and knowledge develop in the nutrient-rich soil of education and training. To fully grasp their area, entrepreneurs must investigate a variety of possibilities, including formal schooling, online courses, and workshops.

Formal Education and Degrees: Traditional education offers a thorough comprehension of fundamental ideas and theories, such as bachelor's or master's degrees in pertinent subjects. Through projects and case studies, formal education delivers structured learning that frequently has real-world implications. Entrepreneurs looking to establish a solid foundation for their entrepreneurial careers may choose formal education if they want in-depth information and academic certifications.

Online Courses and Certifications: Numerous online learning platforms that offer specialized courses and certifications have emerged with the advent of the digital era. Access to courses given by professionals in the field is made possible through websites like Coursera, edX, and LinkedIn Learning. These courses focus on abilities and subjects, enabling business owners to pick up specialized knowledge at their own speed. Certifications increase credibility in the targeted niche by validating knowledge.

Workshops, Seminars, and Bootcamps: Bootcamps, seminars, and workshops offer in-depth, practical learning opportunities. These intensive courses emphasize practical abilities and encourage students to work in teams to solve problems as they arise. Industry experts frequently serve as workshop facilitators, sharing knowledge on current trends and best practices. By taking part, you can develop your skills in a fun, engaging setting.

## Gaining Practical Experience Through Internships and Freelancing: Bridging Theory and Practice

Real-world experiences serve as a link between theoretical understanding and practical skills. Entrepreneurs have the chance to put their abilities to use in real-world, professional settings through internships and freelancing opportunities.

Internships: A systematic setting is offered by internships for applying academic knowledge to practical situations. Interns get hands-on experience in their chosen fields while working with professionals. Internships expose students to business procedures, group dynamics, and client interactions. Internships teach a variety of skills, from technical mastery to communication and problem-solving abilities.

Freelancing and Side Projects: Entrepreneurs can take on independent initiatives while freelancing and working with clients on a contractual basis. Essential abilities including time management, client communication, and project delivery are developed by freelancers. Side projects offer opportunities for experimentation and creativity, whether performed voluntarily or for personal fulfillment. Entrepreneurs can experiment with new ideas and talents while honing their skills in a low-risk setting.

Entrepreneurial Incubators and Accelerators: Startups and early-stage entrepreneurs might benefit from the immersion programs offered by entrepreneurial incubators and accelerators. These programs offer networking opportunities, resources, and mentoring. Entrepreneurs-in-residence collaborate closely with knowledgeable mentors to learn about their industry. The practical advice of business specialists in the field speeds up the development of skills and business knowledge.

## Case Studies of Skills Development Leading to Entrepreneurial Success

Elon Musk: Mastering Diverse Skills for Innovation

Elon Musk, the brilliant businessman behind brands like Tesla, SpaceX, and Neuralink, is a prime example of the value of developing a wide range of abilities. With a background in both physics and economics, Musk revolutionized several different businesses. His career has been greatly influenced by his capacity to comprehend intricate technical topics and combine them with creative conceptions. Engineering, programming, design, and business strategy are all areas of expertise for Musk. His diverse abilities allow him to spearhead ground-breaking projects, illustrating the value of ongoing education and skill improvement for entrepreneurship.

## Sara Blakely: Embracing Creativity and Persistence

The creator of Spanx, Sara Blakely, set out on her entrepreneurial path armed with ingenuity, tenacity, and a deep awareness of her target market. With a background in sales and communication, Blakely noticed a void in the underwear market. Her revolutionary shapewear design satisfied the needs of ladies looking for cozy, practical solutions thanks to her inventiveness. As a result of Blakely's tenacity and skillful product marketing, Spanx has become a household name. Her business success is a testament to the transforming power of combining creativity, niche awareness, and perseverance in skill development.

## Mark Zuckerberg: Coding Expertise and Adaptability

The co-founder of Facebook (now Meta Platforms, Inc.), Mark Zuckerberg, is an expert programmer with a broad knowledge of technology. Because of his programming skills, he was able to create the first iteration of Facebook, turning a student project into a major global social media hub. The capacity to adapt and never stop learning allowed Zuckerberg to successfully navigate the rapidly changing technological environment. He adopted abilities including product development, leadership, and strategic vision, driving Facebook through important growth and acquisitions. The success of Zuckerberg's business operations highlights the value of technological know-how, flexibility, and strategic abilities.

# Empowering Entrepreneurial Journeys Through Skills Development

Entrepreneurial dreams are transformed into real accomplishments through the catalyst of skill development. Curiosity, commitment, and a constant search for knowledge characterize the transition from novice to expert. The road map to mastering a selected niche includes determining the requisite abilities, looking into various educational possibilities, and getting practical experience. Entrepreneurs must recognize that developing their talents is a lifelong effort and that expertise is a dynamic field that is constantly expanding.

Elon Musk, Sara Blakely, and Mark Zuckerberg's case studies act as lighthouses, exposing the revolutionary potential of skill development. These businesspeople developed a variety of skills while continuously changing and growing their knowledge. They did not merely rely on natural abilities. Their experiences demonstrate how important diverse knowledge, flexibility, and inventive problem-solving are to the success of entrepreneurs.

To succeed in their skill-building endeavors, aspiring entrepreneurs must foster their enthusiasm and curiosity. They must see obstacles as chances for progress and failures as stepping stones on the path to mastery. The essence of entrepreneurship, and skills development shapes inventive thinking, resilience, and flexibility. It is not merely a means to an end. By honing their talents, business owners equip themselves to successfully negotiate the complexities of their industry, turning obstacles into chances and aspirations into thriving enterprises.

Skills are more than simply tools in the dynamic world of entrepreneurship; they provide businesspeople the wings to soar to new heights of impact and innovation. Skills development is more than simply a procedure; it is the transforming force that enables business owners to leave a lasting impression on their respective fields and the wider world. Entrepreneurs who see the revolutionary potential of skill development set out on journeys that are not only professionally satisfying but also profoundly enjoyable. In doing so, they help to create a future in which innovation and competence coexist, paving the way for a legacy of enduring success and transformative effect.

# Chapter 6

# Testing Your Ideas:
# Minimum Viable Product (MVP)

Ideas are the seeds from which strong enterprises grow in the dynamic world of entrepreneurship. However, the process of turning an idea into a profitable business takes a methodical strategy that entails validating, honing, and iterating on these concepts. The idea of the Minimum Viable Product (MVP) is one of the most important approaches in this entrepreneurial process. Developing a minimum viable product or service, performing pilot tests to obtain input, and iteratively fine-tuning offers based on feedback and market response are all significant components of this chapter's incisive analysis of the MVP strategy. Entrepreneurs may negotiate the challenges of finding their niche by using this strategic framework, which will also help them transform their initial ideas into strong, customer-focused businesses.

## Developing a Minimum Viable Product or Service: The Birth of Innovation

The key idea behind the MVP strategy is to keep things simple by developing a basic version of the good or service that contains the main selling point. The MVP acts as the cornerstone around which business owners construct their understanding of the market, enabling them to test hypotheses, acquire information, and come to wise judgments.

Identifying Core Features: The first step in creating an MVP is to determine the key characteristics that characterize the good or service. These characteristics serve as the product's distinctive selling factors and focus on the target market's primary problems. Entrepreneurs must reduce their concept to its essentials, concentrating on functionality that is directly related to the central value proposition.

Prototyping and Development: Making a functional but simplified prototype of a good or service is known as prototyping. For digital goods, this can entail creating a streamlined app or website with the core functions. Entrepreneurs can build prototypes for tangible things utilizing easily available materials. Functionality is prioritized overlooks, allowing business owners to save resources while gauging the sustainability of their projects.

Lean Development Principles: The lean development ideals of efficiency, quick iteration, and resource optimization are strongly matched with the MVP strategy. Lean approaches are used by business owners to simplify the development process by getting rid of extraneous features and complexities. By using a lean methodology, the MVP is created quickly and with few resources, allowing business owners to concentrate on validating their hypotheses and obtaining feedback.

## Conducting Pilot Tests and Gathering Feedback: The Crucible of Validation

Pilot tests act as a testing ground for concepts, assumptions, and feedback, which entrepreneurs use as a lighthouse. In these tests, the MVP is made available to a small number of users or clients, enabling business owners to witness actual user interactions and gain insightful information.

Targeted User Groups: Entrepreneurs pinpoint user groups or demographics that fit their intended market. These teams act as the MVP's initial testers. Entrepreneurs may decide to target early adopters, current clients, or people who fit the profile of their ideal client. Targeted user groups guarantee that input is pertinent and offer details on the tastes and habits of the desired market.

User Experience and Feedback Collection: Entrepreneurs concentrate on studying user interactions with the MVP while doing pilot tests. They gather user experience data, including usability, functionality, and general satisfaction. Direct observation, usability testing, interviews, surveys, and other methods can all be used to gather this input. Entrepreneurs closely examine user preferences, pain issues, and improvement suggestions. Entrepreneurs are guided by user input to improve their offerings in response to current market demands.

Iterative Feedback Loops: Iterative feedback loops are started by the feedback obtained during pilot tests. Entrepreneurs review the feedback, spot trends, and list areas that need the most work. They refine the MVP iteratively, considering certain user concerns. Due to the quick iterative cycles, business owners can quickly improve their offers. The ongoing feedback loops guarantee that the MVP changes in response to customer and market feedback, ensuring that the ultimate good or service closely matches customer expectations.

## Iterative Refinement of Your Offerings Based on Feedback and Market Response: The Path to Market Fit

The MVP technique is known for its iterative refinement process. Entrepreneurs create a continual loop of improvement by modifying their offers in response to the input they receive from pilot tests. The best possible alignment between the needs of the market and the product or service is achieved through iterative refinement, which is the key to attaining product-market fit.

Feature Prioritization and Enhancement: Entrepreneurs emphasize the features and functionalities that are most important to users based on user input. Enhancements are made to features that are popular and meet user needs, while less important aspects could be scrapped or given another look. Resource allocation is made more effective by focusing on features that significantly improve the user experience and value proposition.

<u>User-Centric Design and Experience</u>: Entrepreneurs employ user-centric design techniques to make sure the minimum viable product (MVP) is intuitive, user-friendly, and meets user expectations. The design of user interfaces and user experiences (UI/UX) is crucial to the iterative refinement process. To produce user interfaces that are aesthetically pleasing, simple to use, and increase overall user pleasure, entrepreneurs iterate on the design while taking customer feedback into account.

<u>Scaling Responsibility</u>: Entrepreneurs must get ready for scaling while the MVP is iteratively improved. Iterative feedback loops make sure that the product or service is reliable and addresses the needs and problems of users. When scaling, care is taken to match the operational procedures, customer service, and infrastructure to the changing needs of the market. While the client base grows, the quality of the offering is maintained through responsible scaling.

## MVP Success Stories

<u>Dropbox: Iterative Evolution from MVP to Market Leader</u>

A successful MVP is Dropbox, a company that was launched in 2007 by Drew Houston and Arash Ferdowsi. The first iteration of Dropbox embodied the fundamental idea of cloud-based file synchronization and served as a simple file-sharing and storage solution. Users could easily upload and exchange files thanks to the founders' straightforward MVP, which they developed to test their concept. The creators decided to invest in iterative improvement after receiving positive feedback on the MVP. Dropbox implemented functions including file versioning, selective syncing, and collaborative sharing in response to user recommendations and comments. By using an iterative process, Dropbox was able to continuously improve and become a market leader in cloud storage and collaboration tools.

## Instagram: From Prototype to social media Giant

Instagram began as a basic photo-sharing software when it was first created in 2010 by Kevin Systrom and Mike Krieger. With a focus on usability and networking, the founders created an MVP that allowed users to post and exchange photographs. The MVP perfectly encapsulated social involvement and visual storytelling. The appeal of photo filters and convenient sharing tools was underscored by user comments. In line with user feedback, Instagram adopted incremental refinement, adding filters, hashtags, and location tagging to the app. Instagram's precipitous rise was facilitated by the ongoing user experience improvement and the incorporation of cutting-edge technologies, which finally resulted in its acquisition by Facebook in 2012.

## Buffer: Listening to Users for Continuous Improvement

The MVP strategy was used by Buffer, a social media management platform launched by Joel Gascoigne and

Leo Widrich in 2010, to develop a user-friendly scheduling tool. Buffer's early iteration lets users plan out their social media posts. User input was crucial to Buffer's iterative improvement. The creators of Buffer actively sought out customer feedback and preferences, which resulted in the inclusion of features like statistics, group collaboration, and personalized scheduling. Buffer developed into a comprehensive social media management tool that is acclaimed for its simplicity and efficiency by actively listening to users and meeting their demands.

## The MVP Approach as the Beacon of Entrepreneurial Success

The MVP strategy serves as a beacon in the dynamic world of entrepreneurship, pointing prospective businesspeople in the direction of long-term success. Entrepreneurs convert vague ideas into concrete, saleable products, or services by creating a minimally viable product or service, running pilot tests, and embracing incremental development. The MVP strategy ensures that entrepreneurial endeavors are based on the needs and preferences of the audience by embodying the spirit of adaptability, reactivity, and customer-centricity.

The case studies of Dropbox, Instagram, and Buffer shed light on the MVP approach's transformative potential. These businesses did more than just produce goods; they also nourished concepts, checked presumptions, and improved their services in response to immediate customer input. Their responsiveness, ingenuity, and dedication to customer pleasure were demonstrated by the iterative path from MVP to market-ready solution.

Entrepreneurs starting along the road of niche discovery must understand the MVP strategy as a tactical compass. It is a mindset that places a high value on learning, adaptation, and customer empathy rather than just a methodology. The MVP strategy encourages business owners to see opportunities in uncertainty, value feedback as a valuable resource, and consider obstacles as opportunities for innovation.

Entrepreneurs who use the MVP strategy engage on a transformative journey where ideas are molded, improved, and elevated rather than just tested. The MVP approach is the essence of entrepreneurship itself—a continuous cycle of creation, validation, and progress. It is not simply one stage in the entrepreneurial process.

Entrepreneurs who choose the MVP strategy set out on a transformative voyage where ideas come to life under the guidance of user input and market trends. The MVP strategy, which drives entrepreneurs to the peak of success, is more than just a methodology. It is the beating heart of innovation. The MVP approach is the thread that turns visions into reality in the tapestry of entrepreneurial initiatives, resulting in businesses that are not only visionary but also deeply influential and resonate with the needs and ambitions of the market. A future where innovation has no bounds and customer happiness is vital will be shaped by entrepreneurs who use the MVP approach, and who discover not just their niche but also the long-lasting path to entrepreneurial brilliance. In this future, ideas will be fostered through the iterative journey of MVP, becoming the cornerstone of transformative ventures, and leaving an indelible mark on industries, communities, and the entrepreneurial landscape.

# Chapter 7

# Building Your Brand: Communicating Your Unique Selling Proposition (USP)

Building a brand that stands out is crucial in the huge commercial world, where competition is stiff and customer options are plentiful. A brand represents a company's identity, values, and promises; it is more than just a logo or a product. The emotional connection is what turns sporadic patrons into devoted supporters. Entrepreneurs must master the skill of creating a Unique Selling Proposition (USP) and an authentic brand story if they want to find their market and make a lasting impression. In-depth discussions about developing a USP, a compelling brand narrative, and a genuine personal brand that resonates strongly with the target audience are the focus of this chapter. By doing these crucial actions, business owners can successfully negotiate the competitive landscape and build brands that transform their industries and the hearts of their customers, in addition to being memorable and recognizable.

## Defining Your Unique Selling Proposition (USP): The Essence of Distinction

Every successful company has a Unique Selling Proposition (USP), which is a distinguishing argument that persuades consumers to choose it over rival products. The USP captures the distinctive value that a brand provides to its consumers, differentiating it from rivals and providing a strong reason for customers to interact.

<u>Identifying Core Strengths</u>: Understanding the main strengths of the company is the cornerstone of a USP. Entrepreneurs must pinpoint their strengths, whether they are unrivaled quality, exceptional customer service, creative solutions, or reasonable prices. The cornerstones of the USP are these fundamental strengths.

<u>Understanding Customer Needs</u>: The target audience's particular demands and desires are in line with a strong USP. Entrepreneurs need to carry out in-depth market research, talking to clients to find out about their preferences and unmet needs. Understanding client views allows business owners to modify their USP to specifically address these issues, resulting in a solution that resonates strongly with the target market.

<u>Analyzing Competition</u>: Crafting a unique proposition requires doing a comparative investigation of competitors. Entrepreneurs must evaluate the products and services of rivals in the specialized market to find any weaknesses or opportunities for their brand to shine. Entrepreneurs can develop a USP that highlights their unique selling proposition by pitching their company as a remedy for current market weaknesses.

## Crafting a Compelling Brand Story: The Narrative of Connection

A brand story creates an emotional bond between the brand and its audience that goes beyond the features and advantages. A great story elevates a business from being just a supplier of goods or services to becoming a personable, memorable character in the eyes of customers.

Embracing Authenticity: An effective brand story is built on authenticity. Entrepreneurs must incorporate real experiences, values, and drives into their narratives. Consumers respond strongly to genuine stories because they feel more trusted and relatable. The brand becomes more approachable and appealing to the audience when it has a genuine brand story.

Creating Emotional Resonance: The use of emotion in storytelling is effective. Consumers are more likely to remember a brand story that makes them feel something, whether it's inspiration, empathy, nostalgia, or delight. Entrepreneurs may develop stories that address universal topics and elicit strong emotional reactions from a broad audience. Customers are more likely to interact with a business on a deeper level when they feel emotionally connected, which increases loyalty and fosters a sense of belonging.

Showcasing Impact and Values: Consumers in the modern day are becoming more and more aware of how their decisions may affect society and the environment. Brands that support important causes and communicate their beliefs in compelling ways are perceived favorably. In their brand stories, entrepreneurs can emphasize their dedication to social responsibility, sustainability, or community involvement. Entrepreneurs build a narrative that appeals to socially conscious customers by highlighting the good influence their brand has on the world.

## Building an Authentic Personal Brand: The Power of Human Connection

In a time when digital interactions predominate, an entrepreneur's brand is crucial to developing credibility and trust. A genuine personal brand strengthens the overall brand identity as well as the reputation of the individual.

Clarity of Identity: Entrepreneurs need to be aware of who they are as people—their values, beliefs, areas of competence, and distinguishing characteristics. A personal brand is an extension of the person and showcases their true self. Entrepreneurs can use self-analysis and self-discovery to identify their own brand identity.

Consistent Messaging: Building a personal brand requires consistency. Entrepreneurs must make sure that their communications, whether it be in written content, public appearances, or social media, are true to their brand identity. Building credibility and reiterating the authenticity of the personal brand are two benefits of consistent messaging.

<u>Engagement and Accessibility</u>: The development of personal brands requires interaction and accessibility. Through social media channels, business owners may interact with their audience by answering questions, providing knowledge, and taking part in pertinent discussions. A sense of approachability is created by accessibility, both online and off, and it enables customers and followers to establish a personal connection with the business owner.

## Unique Selling Propositions, Brand Stories, and Personal Brand Successes

<u>Apple Inc.: Innovation and Elegance as a USP</u>
Apple Inc. is a perfect example of the effectiveness of innovation and style in a USP. Modern technology, a seamless user experience, and beautiful design make up Apple's USP. Apple has built a position in the industry by continually releasing products that blend cutting-edge technology with simplicity. The brand has a devoted following thanks to its focus on svelte design, clear interfaces, and user-friendly gadgets. Apple's USP goes beyond features and centers on an innovative and elegant attitude that appeals to customers looking for outstanding quality and beauty.

<u>Nike: Empowering Through Inspiration</u>

Nike, a pioneer in athletic footwear and gear worldwide, has created a memorable brand narrative centered on motivation and emancipation. The story of Nike focuses on the journey of athletes, honoring their adversity, success, and commitment. The catchphrase for the company, "Just Do It," captures the attitude of tenacity and fortitude. Nike's brand story motivates people to follow their passions, face obstacles head-on, and excel. Nike has developed a brand that goes beyond its products and becomes a symbol of inspiration and emancipation by connecting its story with the goals of athletes and enthusiasts.

## The Art of Enduring Connection and Influence

It takes skill, a delicate dance of authenticity, inventiveness, and human connection to create a brand that has a lasting emotional impact on the audience. The foundation of brand distinctiveness is the Unique Selling Proposition (USP), which outlines what sets a company apart in consumers' eyes. By adding depth and passion to a tale, a great brand story may captivate audiences. Establishing a genuine personal brand improves credibility and fosters followers' and consumers' loyalty.

Entrepreneurs use their brushstrokes to paint vivid representations of identity, values and promises in the tapestry of brand construction. The capacity to communicate not just superficial details but also a profound essence—a narrative that speaks to the audience's hopes, difficulties, and dreams—is what defines artists. A strong brand is more than simply a logo or a catchphrase; it's an adventure that people take while discovering comfort, inspiration, or delight in the company's products.

The case studies of Nike and Apple Inc. shed light on the practice of enduring impact and connection. These companies created experiences rather than just selling things, evoking feelings, and creating bonds that go beyond business dealings. Not only characteristics, Apple's elegance, Nike's inspiration, and Musk's creativity are the souls of brands that have become cultural phenomena, influencing how people view and interact with the outside world.

The art of brand development must be embraced by entrepreneurs who want to find their niche as a transformative undertaking. It involves storytelling as well as marketing. Emotions are important, too, not just physical characteristics. The impact is more important than just items. Entrepreneurs must go deeply into the soul of their businesses to comprehend the fundamental qualities, principles, and goals that make up their brand. They need to develop stories that are felt, motivate action, and leave a lasting impression.

Entrepreneurs who successfully traverse the brand-building process develop into more than simply company leaders; they also become storytellers who weave tales of creativity, resiliency, and human connection. Entrepreneurs mold perceptions, sway choices, and leave a mark on consumers' hearts through their brands. Creating a legacy of enduring connection, unshakeable trust, and significant influence is at the heart of the art of brand building.

In the vast fabric of entrepreneurship, brands are more than simply things; they are heirlooms that bear witness to the imagination, fervor, and foresight of individuals who dared to imagine and connect. A legacy of brands that not only exist in the market but thrive in people's hearts is created by entrepreneurs through the art of brand building, carving their names into the annals of history and influencing a future where connection, authenticity, and influence are not just aspirations but the very fabric of long-term success and transformative impact.

# Chapter 8

# Networking and Mentorship: Learning from Others

In the fast-paced world of entrepreneurship, finding one's specialty requires constant learning, flexibility, and the capacity to go ahead in new waters. The ability to network well and learn from mentorships are two of the most effective tools available to entrepreneurs. Finding and succeeding in one's niche requires, among other things, developing a professional network within the selected specialty, looking for mentorship from successful businesspeople, and taking lessons from both successes and failures. The transforming effect of networking and mentorship is thoroughly explored in this chapter, shedding light on how these priceless connections influence entrepreneurial journeys and promote long-term success.

## Building a Professional Network Within Your Niche: The Power of Collaboration

A professional network is more than just a list of contacts; it is also a thriving ecology of opportunities, joint ventures, and ideas. Entrepreneurs who invest to develop a strong professional network in their specialized field put themselves at the intersection of innovation and knowledge.

Identifying Key Players: Some people and groups act as linchpins within every niche. These prominent figures could be well-known businesspeople, subject-matter experts, or cutting-edge startups. Entrepreneurs can access a wealth of expertise, get a perception of market trends, and probe prospective alliances by locating and communicating with these people.

Participation in Industry Events and Conferences: Industry gatherings and conferences provide excellent networking opportunities. Entrepreneurs can interact with like-minded individuals, present their ventures, and create vital connections at conferences, trade exhibitions, and seminars relating to their sector. These gatherings provide chances for face-to-face communication, fostering deep connections that may result in partnerships and company expansion.

Online Communities and Social Media: Social media platforms and online communities that target niches have emerged because of the digital world. Entrepreneurs can connect with industry specialists by joining relevant forums, LinkedIn groups, and Facebook groups. Enhancing visibility and credibility within the specialty by active involvement in conversations, exchange of thoughts, and interaction with peers. Social media platforms can be used to network with thought leaders and influencers and to build relationships that may lead to new opportunities.

# Seeking Mentorship from Experienced Entrepreneurs: Guided Wisdom for Strategic Growth

In the entrepreneurial sector, mentoring is a time-honored custom that gives mentees the chance to gain knowledge from the experiences, triumphs, and difficulties of seasoned mentors. Entrepreneurs can use a mentor as a compass, guiding them toward strategic growth and well-informed decisions.

Identifying Suitable Mentors: Finding the ideal mentor requires striking a careful balance between complementing skills, respect for one another, and shared ideals. Entrepreneurs should look for mentors who have experience in their specialized field, comprehend the intricacies of the market, and are eager to devote time and energy to supporting the mentee's development. The entrepreneur's professional network, trade shows, or mentorship programs provided by entrepreneurial organizations are all potential sources of mentorship.

Openness to Learning: Openness to learning is essential for successful mentoring. Entrepreneurs should approach mentoring with a modest attitude, prepared to take in advice, criticism, and feedback. Mentorship should be deliberately sought out by mentees as part of a continual learning process, not just during times of need. A dynamic mentor-mentee connection is fostered by a mentee's openness to advice and permits valuable information and wisdom exchanges.

Regular and Meaningful Interactions: Regular and meaningful encounters are the foundation of effective mentoring. Entrepreneurs should set up regular meetings with their mentors to go over problems, get input on tactical choices, and offer updates on their progress. These interactions establish a safe space for mentees to express worries, generate ideas, and get helpful advice from mentors. An informal connection of mutual trust and camaraderie is fostered between mentors and mentees that often develops outside of scheduled meetings.

## Learning from the Success Stories and Failures of Others in Your Niche: Extracting Insights from Experience

A niche's success and failure tales are a priceless source of information. These stories help entrepreneurs develop a comprehensive grasp of market dynamics, tactical options, and potential hazards. Entrepreneurs may make informed judgments and steer clear of frequent pitfalls by learning from the mistakes of others.

Case Studies and Industry Analyses: Case studies and industry assessments offer in-depth insights into the tactics used by profitable niche enterprises. Successful enterprises' growth trajectories, market positions, and competitive advantages can be studied by entrepreneurs. Entrepreneurs can find patterns, novel strategies, and best practices that can be applied to their own companies by studying case studies.

Failure Post-Mortems: Equally illuminating is comprehending a niche's failures. Post-mortems of failed firms provide a direct look at the difficulties encountered, errors made, and lessons learned. Entrepreneurs can learn from failure's contributing aspects so they can proactively manage comparable risks in their future endeavors. Failure post-mortems act as a warning by outlining hazards that business owners should stay away from.

Interviews and Thought Leadership: Successful businesspeople and thought leaders in the specialized field are interviewed to get firsthand perspectives of their experiences. Entrepreneurs can learn about the thought patterns, decision-making techniques, and creative concepts of industry leaders. Thought leaders frequently offer insightful viewpoints through blog posts, podcasts, and public speeches, providing a plethora of information that can motivate and guide business strategies.

# Examples of Networking, Mentorship, and Learning from Others

## Richard Branson: A Network of Innovation and Inspiration

The Virgin Group's founder, Richard Branson, is well known for having a wide network and being able to form effective alliances. Entrepreneurs, opinion leaders, and business executives from a range of industries are part of Branson's network. Branson has enabled partnerships, investments, and business endeavors that have helped the Virgin Group achieve success on a global scale through his vast network. Branson is a prime example of the power of strategic networking because of how well he can forge connections and use his network to further his business enterprises.

Steve Jobs: Learning from Failures and Innovation

Co-founder of Apple Inc. Steve Jobs had several notable successes and significant setbacks during his entrepreneurial career. Jobs learned priceless lessons about invention, leadership, and market dynamics from his early experiences with Apple, including his termination from the firm. After rejoining Apple, Jobs revolutionized the business with ground-breaking devices including the iPod, iPhone, and iPad. Jobs' capacity for adapting to shifting market demands, learning from mistakes, and developing ground-breaking technology served as the cornerstone of Apple's comeback. The entrepreneurial legacy of Jobs is proof of the transformative value of taking lessons from both successes and mistakes.

# The Art of Collective Wisdom

The entrepreneurial art is made up of the collective wisdom, experiences, and insights of those who have traveled the entrepreneurial journey. Threads in this tapestry include networking and mentoring. Entrepreneurs find chances in the complex web of connections, but they also learn important lessons that influence their viewpoints and tactics. By providing access to various ideas and collaborative endeavors, networking broadens horizons. Mentoring fosters progress by giving mentees a compass and sounding board for their strategic decisions. Entrepreneurs have a deep grasp of market dynamics through learning from the triumphs and failures of others, which enables them to make wise, strategic decisions.

The case studies of Steve Jobs, and Richard Branson act as lighthouses, exposing the transformative potential of networking. These businesspeople did not become successful by themselves; rather, they embraced the collective knowledge of their networks, sought mentorship, and learned from the mistakes of others. Their experiences serve as illustrative examples of the value of mentoring, teamwork, and a humble openness to learning in the quest for entrepreneurial achievement.

Entrepreneurs who want to find their niche must understand that networking and mentorship are essential elements of their entrepreneurial journey rather than optional extras. Opportunities, partnerships, and beneficial contacts are made possible by networking. Mentorship acts as a compass, guiding business owners through uncharted waters with the knowledge gained from experience. Understanding other people's triumphs and mistakes provides a holistic viewpoint, enhancing entrepreneurial methods with a variety of ideas.

In this complex web of entrepreneurship, every relationship formed, every mentorship obtained, and every lesson gained becomes a thread—an essential component of the entrepreneur's story. These strands don't just tell a tale; they build a legacy—one of cooperative creativity, guided wisdom, and well-informed choices. In addition to finding their specialization, entrepreneurs who embrace the tapestry of communal wisdom also find their resilience, transformative effect, and a deep sense of purpose.

Entrepreneurs walk hand in hand with the collective knowledge of their networks, mentors, and the experiences of those who have come before them as they traverse the constantly changing environment of their niches. In this shared journey, entrepreneurs discover not only success but also fulfillment. This fulfillment stems from the realization that they are part of a larger tapestry, where each thread, each connection, and each mentorship add to the vibrant mosaic of entrepreneurial innovation and enduring impact, a mosaic that shapes industries, empowers communities, and inspires future generations.

# Chapter 9

# Overcoming Challenges: Building Resilience

Entrepreneurs encounter a variety of difficulties when they seek to identify and succeed in a niche. The voyage is not a straight rise but rather a dynamic exploration with unexpected curves and difficulties. To create a successful niche business, one must recognize opportunities and develop resilience—the capacity to recover from failures, change course when necessary, and come out on top. This chapter explores the art of overcoming obstacles, examining the typical problems that niche firms encounter, the growth of resilience and adaptive abilities, and methods for overcoming failures and setbacks. Entrepreneurs who have a resilient mindset can use obstacles as stepping stones to achieve long-term success in their chosen markets.

## Identifying Common Challenges Faced by Niche Businesses: Navigating the Terrain of Obstacles

Despite their specialization, niche firms are not exempt from difficulties. They frequently run against unusual obstacles that call for creative fixes and unyielding resolve. The first step in creating efficient solutions to overcome these obstacles is recognizing them.

Limited Market Reach: Specialized markets are where niche enterprises operate, which may restrict their clientele. A limited audience makes it difficult to grow the firm and produce a steady income. To attract potential customers outside of their narrow expertise, business owners must develop innovative marketing methods.

Intense Competition: Despite their specificity, niche markets can have intense competition. Businesses in the same category that compete with one another compete for customers' attention and loyalty. To remain competitive in the market, entrepreneurs must differentiate their offerings through distinctive value propositions, outstanding client experiences, and creative strategies.

Technological Advancements: Rapid technology improvements have the potential to destroy niche industries with slow adaptability. New technology may affect market dynamics, modify consumer tastes, or make obsolete current goods and services. Entrepreneurs need to stay on top of technology developments and embrace innovation to improve their products and remain competitive.

Economic Volatility: Because of the sensitivity of niche industries to economic changes, consumer purchasing patterns may be affected. The demand for specialty goods and services may decline during economic downturns or recessions. To weather economic storms, entrepreneurs must build their financial resiliency, diversify their sources of income, and put cost-effective strategies into action.

# Developing Resilience and Adaptability Skills: The Foundation of Overcoming Challenges

Resilience is a skill that may be developed and refined rather than being an innate quality. Through deliberate actions and mental changes, entrepreneurs can increase their resilience and flexibility, empowering them to face obstacles with ingenuity and grit.

Embracing a Growth Mindset: According to psychologist Carol Dweck, a growth mindset is the idea that aptitude and intelligence can be developed with commitment and effort. Entrepreneurs who have a growth mentality see difficulties as chances for development. They are resilient in the face of obstacles and accept failures as useful learning experiences.

Cultivating Emotional Intelligence: Effective communication, self-awareness, and empathy are all parts of emotional intelligence. Entrepreneurs with high emotional intelligence can handle difficult situations with grace, comprehend other people's viewpoints, and form effective working partnerships. Entrepreneurs who possess emotional intelligence are more resilient because they are better able to control their stress levels, evolve with the times, and uphold healthy relationships with stakeholders.

Building a Supportive Network: The basis of resilience is a strong support system. Entrepreneurs can surround themselves with supporting friends, family, mentors, peers, and advisers. A supporting network offers inspiration, a range of viewpoints, and insightful information. Entrepreneurs can rely on their network for support, counsel, and emotional assistance during difficult times.

Practicing Mindfulness and Stress Management: Yoga and meditation are examples of mindfulness techniques that improve emotional control, focus, and mental clarity. Entrepreneurs may manage stress, develop resilience, and nurture a sense of serenity despite setbacks by incorporating mindfulness into their daily routines. Exercise, hobbies, and relaxation are all effective stress-reduction strategies that improve general well-being and the capacity to handle challenges with composure.

## Strategies for Overcoming Setbacks and Failures in Your Niche: Turning Challenges into Opportunities

The entrepreneurial journey will always involve setbacks and disappointments. Entrepreneurs' capacity to overcome obstacles and advance toward their goals, however, depends on how they react to these setbacks. Resilience, adaptability, and a proactive approach to problem-solving are strategies for overcoming setbacks.

Learning from Failures: Failures are excellent teaching tools. Entrepreneurs can evaluate the causes of failures, spot areas for development, and take corrective action. Entrepreneurs can gain insights, improve tactics, and prevent future mistakes by adopting a reflective approach.

Pivoting and Innovation: Entrepreneurs might change their strategies or innovate their products in response to obstacles. To respond to changed market demands, pivoting entails adjusting the business strategy, target market, or product/service offerings. Innovation is the process of creating new goods, services, or features to meet changing consumer demands. Entrepreneurs may be adaptable, adjust to market changes, and take advantage of changing possibilities by both pivoting and innovating.

Strategic Collaboration and Partnerships: Partnerships and joint ventures can help find answers to problems. Entrepreneurs can work together with companies, professionals, or groups inside or outside of their specialized fields. Strategic alliances can increase resources, expand market penetration, and capitalize on complementary qualities. Collaboration encourages creativity and invention, which helps people come up with fresh answers to problems.

Customer-Centric Approach: The key to overcoming obstacles is to have a customer-centric strategy. Entrepreneurs can actively seek client feedback, comprehend their demands, and adjust their services as a result. Entrepreneurs increase client pleasure and loyalty by matching products and services to customer preferences. Engaging with customers promotes a sense of community, turning setbacks into chances to forge deeper bonds and increase brand loyalty.

# Case Studies of Resilience in Overcoming Challenges

## Netflix: Adapting to Technological Shifts and Changing Preferences

With the rise of online streaming services, Netflix—originally a DVD rental service—faced difficulties. The corporation quickly changed its business strategy after realizing that consumer tastes were shifting toward online streaming. Netflix invested in the creation of original content and now provides users with exclusive TV shows and films. Netflix evolved from a DVD rental service into a major global streaming force by adjusting to technological advancements and consumer behavior. Netflix is a leader in the entertainment sector thanks to its adaptability and tenacity.

## Slack: Transforming Challenges into Innovation

The popular communication tools were a threat to the team collaboration platform Slack. Slack concentrated on user experience and innovation to stand out. The platform featured user-friendly interfaces, intuitive features, and interactions with outside applications. Slack's extensive popularity in workplaces can be attributed to both its responsiveness to user feedback and its dedication to ongoing improvement. Slack became a popular option for team communication and collaboration because of the company's ability to innovate despite competition.

## The Triumph of Resilience in the Entrepreneurial Journey

Challenges are not obstacles in the complex world of entrepreneurship, but rather chances for development, creativity, and change. Entrepreneurial resilience is the capacity to bounce back from setbacks, adjust to shifting conditions, and grow stronger as a result. Entrepreneurs who are resilient move forward despite challenges because resilience is an active force rather than a passive quality.

Entrepreneurs who practice resilience see obstacles as stimuli for innovation and reinvention. They use the lessons they gain from mistakes to improve their strategy and products. They embrace setbacks as stepping stones toward success. Resilient entrepreneurs have the fortitude to endure difficulties, the flexibility to change course when necessary, and the confidence to face challenges with optimism.

The case studies of Netflix, and Slack show how perseverance triumphs in the venture of entrepreneurship. These businesses faced difficulties head-on and overcame them with creativity, tenacity, and a focus on the consumer. Their experiences support the idea that obstacles, no matter how formidable, can be turned into chances for innovation and advancement.

Entrepreneurs who want to find their niche must internalize resilience's core principles. It is more than just a strategy for surviving; it is a mentality that views obstacles as opportunities for creativity, mistakes as lessons in disguise, and losses as stepping stones to victories. Resilient entrepreneurs do not shy away from difficulties; rather, they view them as allies in the thrilling journey that is entrepreneurship. They see obstacles as collaborators in the creation of their entrepreneurial narratives, helping to define their identities, hone their tactics, and harden their resolve rather than as enemies.

Resilience is not simply a thread in the entrepreneurial tapestry; it is the shining golden filament that illuminates the whole thing. Every successful business depends on it. It is the unseen power that propels development and the unbreakable spirit that characterizes the entrepreneurial spirit. Entrepreneurs who practice resilience don't just get by with problems; they overcome them and come out the other side stronger, wiser, and more resilient.

Resilience is more than just a quality in the epic voyage of entrepreneurial odysseys; it is the anthem of triumph, one that reverberates with every obstacle overcome, every setback overcome, and every ambition fulfilled. Entrepreneurs who practice resilience leave a legacy of tenacity, innovation, and unwavering spirit. This legacy motivates future generations to face challenges head-on, turn setbacks into victories, and start their businesses with the unwavering conviction that resilience is not just quality but the very foundation of long-term success and transformative impact.

# Chapter 10

# Scaling Your Niche Business: Long-Term Growth Strategies

Resilience is more than just a quality in the epic voyage of entrepreneurial odysseys; it is the anthem of triumph, one that reverberates with every obstacle overcome, every setback overcome, and every ambition fulfilled. Entrepreneurs who practice resilience leave a legacy of tenacity, innovation, and unwavering spirit. This legacy motivates future generations to face challenges head-on, turn setbacks into victories, and start their businesses with the unwavering conviction that resilience is not just quality but the very foundation of long-term success and transformative impact.

## Scaling Your Business While Maintaining Your Niche Focus: The Art of Strategic Expansion

A fine balance must be struck to preserve a niche's core values while growing the business. Even as the company expands, the distinct value offer that characterizes a niche must endure. Strategic growth within the specialized market guarantees that the company may serve a wider clientele while maintaining its unique offerings.

Understanding Core Values and Unique Selling Proposition (USP): During expansion, the niche's defining principles and USP must act as a compass. Entrepreneurs should recognize the unique characteristics of their specialized business and make sure these characteristics are maintained as the company grows. These distinguishing qualities—whether they are unmatched quality, individualized services, or cutting-edge solutions—must be incorporated into the expansion strategy.

Segmentation and Targeting: There are frequently several segments with unique demands and preferences within the niche. By recognizing these niches and adjusting their offers to meet customer needs, entrepreneurs may scale their enterprises. Entrepreneurs can create niche-specific product/service versions that appeal to various client demographics by understanding the subtleties of the market's various customer segments.

Strategic Alliances and Partnerships: Strategic expansion might be facilitated by partnerships with other companies and organizations operating in the niche. Entrepreneurs can investigate collaborations that strengthen their value proposition, broaden their market reach, and complement their offers. Strategic partnerships can result in co-branded goods, joint marketing campaigns, or resource sharing, allowing specialist enterprises to grow without losing sight of their primary objectives.

## Leveraging Technology and Automation for Efficiency: The Digital Transformation Advantage

Technology is a powerful engine for growing enterprises in the digital age. Utilizing technology and automation not only increases productivity but also gives specialized firms the adaptability they need to meet changing client and market expectations.

E-commerce and Online Platforms: Adopting e-commerce and internet platforms opens opportunities to a worldwide customer base for niche firms. With the help of online marketplaces, business owners can reach a larger audience and encourage clients to make purchases from any location in the world. To improve the consumer experience, e-commerce platforms also provide services including safe payment gateways, order tracking, and tailored recommendations.

Data Analytics and Market Insights: Tools for data analytics provide niche enterprises with useful insights. Entrepreneurs may make educated decisions about product offers, marketing plans, and customer engagement initiatives by examining customer behavior, preferences, and trends. Businesses may improve customer happiness, manage operations, and find fresh chances for market expansion with the help of data-driven insights.

Automation and Process Optimization: Internal procedures are streamlined through automation, which also reduces human labor and minimizes error. Tasks like order processing, inventory management, customer assistance, and marketing campaigns can all be automated by niche enterprises. In addition to increasing efficiency, automation also frees up resources, enabling business owners and staff to concentrate on strategic initiatives, innovation, and consumer interactions.

## Expanding Your Niche Offerings and Exploring Related Markets: Diversification and Sustained Growth

Even though keeping a niche focus is crucial, adjacent opportunities frequently exist within linked areas. Businesses can diversify their revenue sources, reduce risk, and take advantage of synergies by growing their specialized product offerings and investigating connected markets.

Product Line Extensions: By providing additional goods or services, business owners can broaden the scope of their specialized offers. A skincare-focused niche beauty brand might, for instance, launch a line of cosmetics or accessories. Product line expansions serve current clients while luring in new ones looking for all-inclusive solutions in the market.

Vertical Integration: Expanding activities across several supply chain stages is referred to as vertical integration. By acquiring or collaborating with suppliers, manufacturers, or distributors who are also in the specialty, niche enterprises can study vertical integration. Vertical integration ensures a strong and effective supply chain by improving control over quality, lowering costs, and fostering seamless collaboration.

<u>Horizontal Expansion into Related Markets</u>: Niche companies can consider horizontal expansion into similar markets that complement their core products. For instance, a niche organic food company can investigate sectors like eco-friendly home goods, health supplements, or sustainable packaging. When pursuing new growth opportunities, firms can take advantage of existing knowledge, reputation, and client base through horizontal expansion.

## Examples of Scaling Niche Businesses

<u>Blue Apron: Diversifying Offerings Within the Meal Kit Niche</u>

A meal kit delivery service called Blue Apron fills a market need for gastronomic ease. Blue Apron expanded its product line while keeping its emphasis on meal kits by creating specialty plans that catered to various dietary needs, such as vegetarian and wellness-focused meals. The business also entered alliances with well-known chefs, releasing special dishes that were more broadly appealing. By strategically diversifying, Blue Apron was able to grow within its market segment while maintaining its core focus on culinary innovation and convenience.

<u>Casper: Horizontal Expansion into Sleep-Related Products</u>

Initially a specialized mattress-in-a-box firm, Casper has grown horizontally into adjacent sleep-related markets. Casper created a variety of sleep-related items, including pillows, sheets, and sleep-tracking gadgets, by utilizing its experience in sleep technology. The business also considered joint ventures with hotel chains and other lodging establishments, offering its goods for a relaxing and enjoyable stay for visitors. Casper's horizontal development enabled the company to grow while leveraging its specialized knowledge of improving sleep quality.

Peleton: Vertical Integration and Community Building

Vertical integration and community-building tactics were embraced by Peloton, a specialized fitness firm that specializes in linked training equipment. The business manufactures treadmills and exercise cycles in addition to providing a subscription-based content platform with live and recorded fitness programs. Peloton vertically integrated its business operations to guarantee flawless software and hardware integration. By enabling people to take part in live lessons and compete against other users, Peloton also promoted a sense of community among its users. The social component increased consumer loyalty and engagement, helping Peloton to grow inside the linked fitness market.

# The Harmonious Symphony of Focus and Expansion

Scaling a niche firm is a symphony of focus and expansion—a musical fusion of keeping the niche's character while looking for growth opportunities. Entrepreneurs must learn how to balance strategically broadening their horizons while keeping their fundamental principles and distinctive services. The trick is in knowing how diversification and focus are interconnected and that niche essence should be enhanced, not diluted.

Entrepreneurship is a dynamic field where specialty enterprises are living, evolving organisms that change, adapt, and thrive. Scaling inside a niche requires more than just entrepreneurial zeal; it also requires brilliant market and strategic judgment. Scaling entrepreneurs negotiate the challenges of growth with skill, ensuring that their niche firms thrive as market leaders and consumer favorites.

Entrepreneurs must adopt a diversified strategy as they set out on the path to scaling their niche enterprises. While strategically expanding presents potential for income diversification and market supremacy, maintaining a narrow focus gives the company a distinctive brand and a devoted customer base. Utilizing automation and technology improves operational effectiveness, ensuring that the company is flexible and responsive to market demands. Entrepreneurs can take advantage of synergies and expand their reach by investigating related markets and expanding their services, capturing new market niches.

Entrepreneurs run their businesses with precision and vision amid the symphony of focus and expansion. They combine the melody of innovation, customer centricity, and strategic partnerships to produce a work that appeals to a wide range of viewers. The entrepreneurial symphony is a composition that inspires future generations to strike the chords of focus and expansion and create their own harmonious Odysseys of discovery, growth, and transformative success. It is more than just an orchestration of goods and services; it is a masterpiece of vision, adaptability, and lasting impact.

# Conclusion

Finding your niche is like finding your true north in the maze of entrepreneurial exploration—a guiding star that shows the way to a successful firm. The process of finding a niche is more than just a procedure; it is a transforming odyssey that travels through the regions of self-discovery, market alignment, and creative strategy. It is crucial to evaluate, celebrate, and take the first significant measures toward your entrepreneurial aspirations as you stand at the beginning of your specialty journey and are prepared to begin the thrilling experience of developing a firm founded on your passions and talents.

## Reflecting on Your Niche Discovery Process: The Quest for Authenticity

Your niche discovery method, an introspective journey that explores the depths of your passions, abilities, and objectives, is a testimonial to your genuineness. Thinking back on this process is like looking into a mirror that not only shows your picture but also your essence—an essence infused with the fire of your dreams and the sincerity of your personality.

<u>Self-Exploration and Passion Mapping</u>: You went on a deep exploration of your passions while searching for your specialty. You dug deep into your areas of expertise, interests, and hobbies to find the threads that woven your

enthusiasm together. Finding the intersections between your interests and areas of competence was revealed because of mapping out your passions.

Market Alignment and Opportunity Recognition: Your method of identifying your specialty went beyond self-examination to include market research and opportunity awareness. You researched industry trends, found gaps, and ascertained the requirements and goals of your target market. It wasn't only a strategic decision to match your interests with market demands; it was also a harmonious union where your distinctive products found resonance with the needs of your target market.

Clarity of Vision and Purpose: You gained clarity of vision and purpose via the process of discovering your specialization. You explained why you do what you do as well as what you do. Your vision turned into a lighthouse that helped you navigate the complexities of business decisions. Your mission served as the engine that drove you resolutely toward your objectives. This clarity is more than simply a light; it is a cornerstone, and it will serve as the foundation for your entrepreneurial legacy.

## Celebrating Your Unique Strengths and Passions: The Symphony of Self-Appreciation

It is not vain to celebrate your talents and interests; rather, doing so is an expression of gratitude for the incredible array of traits that make you who you are. Your abilities to overcome obstacles, come up with novel solutions, and motivate others are superpowers, not just skills. Your passions are not just interests; they are ardent flames that stoke your imagination, bolster your resolve, and enlighten your way.

Recognizing Your Unique Strengths: Your entrepreneurship skill is built on your strengths. Each of your strengths—creativity, analytical prowess, communication prowess, leadership traits, etc.—adds to the patchwork of your business identity. Recognizing these talents entails more than only admitting them; it also involves embracing them and celebrating the skills that make you unique and enable success.

Embracing Your Passions as Catalysts for Innovation: Your interests are more than just pastimes; they serve as engines for invention. You give life to your offerings when you incorporate your passions into your business. Your excitement spreads to others, capturing them and winning them over. Instead of just integrating, embracing your passions is energizing—a celebration of the limitless vigor and creativity that drive your entrepreneurial pursuits.

Honoring Your Journey and Growth: Your search for your specialization is a tapestry made of experiences, obstacles, and personal development. Your perseverance and wisdom have evolved with each step, each obstacle, and each victory. Honoring this journey involves more than just reflecting; it also involves relishing in your entrepreneurial evolution and the lessons that have shaped your entrepreneurial spirit.

## Taking the First Steps Toward Building a Successful Business in Your Chosen Niche: The Dawn of Entrepreneurial Triumph

You are not simply an entrepreneur as you prepare to launch your company in your chosen industry; you are also a visionary who creates possibilities and shapes aspirations. The first moves you make are more than just motions; they are turning points in your entrepreneurial legacy. These actions are not just first moves; they are bold assertions of your intention to bring your specific niche vision to life.

Crafting Your Unique Value Proposition: The beating heart of your company is your distinct value proposition. It captures the essence of your niche—your interests, your level of knowledge, and the unique advantages you provide to your clients. Making a statement that resonates with your audience and sets your company apart from the competition is more than just articulating; it also involves enhancing your value offer.

Building Authentic Relationships with Customers: Relationships in the entrepreneur world are partnerships rather than transactions because they are based on honesty, decency, and authenticity. Building genuine connections with your consumers involves more than just communicating with them; it entails creating a bond that goes beyond transactional interactions and promotes loyalty. Customer service pillars include listening to your customers, comprehending their wants, and appreciating their comments. These pillars support the base of sustainable customer relationships.

Embracing Adaptability and Innovation: The entrepreneurial environment is dynamic, and resilience depends on one's capacity to adapt. Embracing adaptation requires more than just flexibility; it also requires vision—a foresight that sees changes in the market and proactively modifies plans. Innovation is evolution—a transformation of your offerings, procedures, and client experiences—rather than just invention. Embracing innovation and flexibility is more than just accepting change; it also means accepting growth, and it means accepting growth that will lead your company to long-term success.

Cultivating a Growth Mindset and Tenacity: Entrepreneurship is not a sprint, but a marathon. Developing a growth mindset requires more than just optimism; it also requires tenacity—tenacity that views obstacles as learning opportunities and setbacks as stepping stones. Tenacity is resilience—a resilience that bounces back from setbacks and perseveres in the face of difficulty. Resilience is more than just persistence. Developing a growth mentality and persistence results in thriving—a thriving that turns challenges into landmarks and ambitions into accomplishments.

# Your Epic Saga of Entrepreneurial Triumph

Do not forget that you are the hero of an epic saga—an odyssey full of twists, victories, and transforming moments—as you embark on your unique quest. Your journey is a record, a narrative of passion, purpose, and the quest for greatness, not simply a chapter. Your story is a legacy in the broad fabric of entrepreneurship—a legacy that inspires, empowers, and makes a permanent mark on the entrepreneurial landscape.

Imagine the tapestry you are weaving as you begin to establish your company in the specific niche you have chosen. This tapestry will be embellished with the brilliant hues of invention, the intricate patterns of client interactions, and the golden threads of your one-of-a-kind value proposition. Every action you do is a brushstroke that paints a picture of your entrepreneurial aspirations on the canvas. Your every choice is a note in the symphony of your achievement. Every obstacle you conquer is a chapter in the epic tale of your resiliency.

Take on your path with boldness, imagination, and unflinching faith in your mission. Honor your passions, celebrate your individuality, and let your entrepreneurial spirit flourish. Your journey is not simply a solo trip; it is a shared adventure with other business owners, aspirational thinkers, and visionaries. You create a community when you come together—a community that values cooperation, embraces difference and supports one another.

Your unique path is more than simply a story in the epic chronicle of entrepreneurial success; it is a legend that inspires future generations by resonating in the halls of inspiration. You are more than just an entrepreneur; you are a lighthouse, a shining example that others can follow as they embark on their entrepreneurial journeys. Your journey is more than just a single event; it is a movement that turns goals into successes and aspirations into realities.

Accept and embrace your specialized journey because it holds the keys to your success, the core of your mission, and the hope for a future fueled by your entrepreneurial genius. Keep in mind that every obstacle is an opportunity, every setback is a preparation for a return, and every desire is a step toward your future.

In your entrepreneurial adventure, you are not simply a participant; you are a legend—a legend in the making. Embrace your niche journey because it is more than just a road; it is a destiny that has been sculpted by your passion, purpose, and unshakeable belief.